World of Science

HEROES

Our Innovators

Written by

Benedict Boo

Illustrated by

Alan Bay

WS Education

NEW JERSEY · LONDON · SINGAPORE · BEIJING · SHANGHAI · HONG KONG · TAIPEI · CHENNAI · TOKYO

Published by

WS Education, an imprint of

World Scientific Publishing Co. Pte. Ltd.

5 Toh Tuck Link, Singapore 596224

USA office: 27 Warren Street, Suite 401-402, Hackensack, NJ 07601

UK office: 57 Shelton Street, Covent Garden, London WC2H 9HE

National Library Board, Singapore Cataloguing in Publication Data
Name(s): Boo, Benedict. | Bay, Alan, illustrator.
Title: Our innovators / written by Benedict Boo ; illustrated by Alan Bay.
Other Title(s): World of science.
Description: Singapore : WS Education, [2024]
Identifier(s): ISBN 978-981-12-7578-4 (hardback) | 978-981-12-7579-1 (paperback) |
    978-981-12-7580-7 (ebook for institutions) | 978-981-12-7581-4 (ebook for individuals)
Subject(s): LCSH: Discoveries in science--Comic books, strips, etc. |
    Discoveries in science--Juvenile literature. | Inventions--Comic books, strips, etc. |
    Inventions--Juvenile literature. | Graphic novels.
Classification: DDC 609--dc23

British Library Cataloguing-in-Publication Data
A catalogue record for this book is available from the British Library.

Printed in Singapore

Meet our Innovators...

Modernisers, creators of new ideas and methods. The individuals in this group are a diverse bunch — rich and poor, men and women, coming from all walks of life. Each one, inspired to make the world better, pursued what seemed to be impossible or unreachable. Their foresight and creativity led to innovations that influenced the society around them and continue to impact many aspects of our lives today.

Peek into the MRI machine with Peter Mansfield. Discover computer language with Grace Hopper. Harness the power of the sun with Maria Telkes. Let our Innovators encourage you to face problems with creative thinking and perseverance!

A Guide to Experiencing the Bonus Features in This Book

See a QR code? Scan it to access bonus resources!

Contents

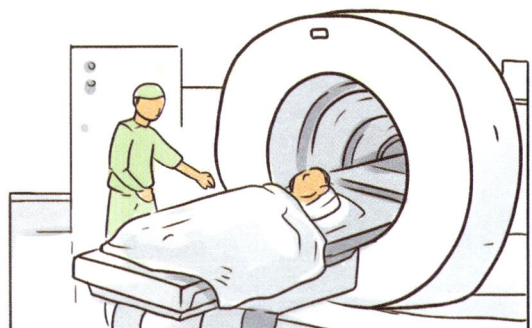

EEEEE—

He Booked Us

6

Cool! So, today's story is about... ME!!

That's right. He's a very special person in history, just like you!

JOHANNES GUTENBERG

Johannes Gutenberg was born to a wealthy family in the German city of Mainz sometime in the 14th Century.

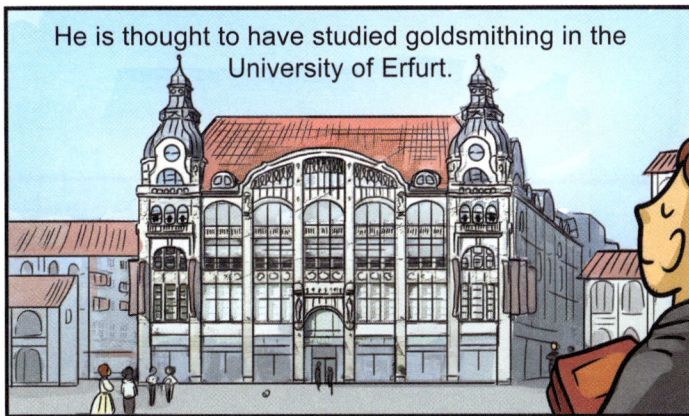

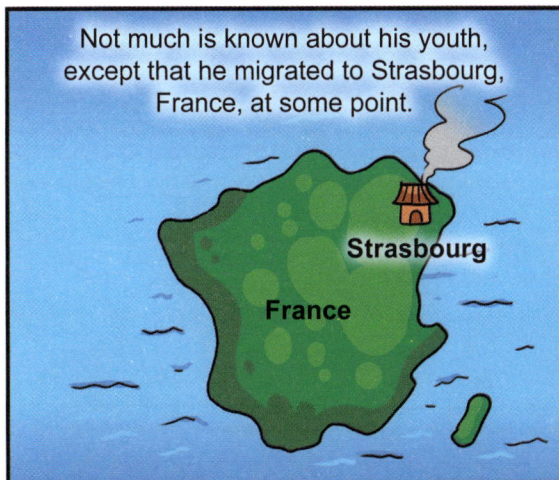

He is thought to have studied goldsmithing in the University of Erfurt.

No, Hans...that is not where they train people to be Bigfoot.

Not much is known about his youth, except that he migrated to Strasbourg, France, at some point.

Strasbourg

France

Some records show that he was a goldsmith apprentice.

Why Strasbourg?

It is believed that Hans migrated to Strasbourg for political reasons. There was an uprising in Mainz, against the noble class. He probably went to Strasbourg, where the family had connections, to escape this disorder in society.

7

He Booked Us

In those days, books were often copied by hand. An error in copying could often change the meaning of a text.

My hand hurts!

Ah, I made a mistake!

Wow! That would require many, many, many people to write all the books!

OR...there just weren't many books around.

That's right. Not many books were available in those days. Those who had books were considered rich and powerful.

So, I guess there were no iPads as well?

Yes, dear. No iPads. Almost all bedtime stories were told from memory. Can you imagine that?

Old Printing Methods

Before the invention of the printing press — sometime between 1440 and 1450 — most European texts were printed using xylography, a form of woodblock printing similar to what the Chinese used. Manuscripts not printed with woodblocks were painstakingly copied by hand.

He Booked Us

In those days, there was a growing demand for books. Johannes Gutenberg researched on a machine that could print books. He recorded his research in a book called *Aventur und Kunst*, meaning "enterprise and art".

JOHANNES GUTENBERG

Did he succeed in the end?

Yes! It is said that he used his knowledge of metal to create blocks of letters for printing.

He created a special ink and adapted a winepress to help him flatten the paper for printing.

By 1450, the Gutenberg Press was ready to start printing!

1450

The printing press helped to eliminate errors made in copying texts.

The books were easier to read and could be produced faster!

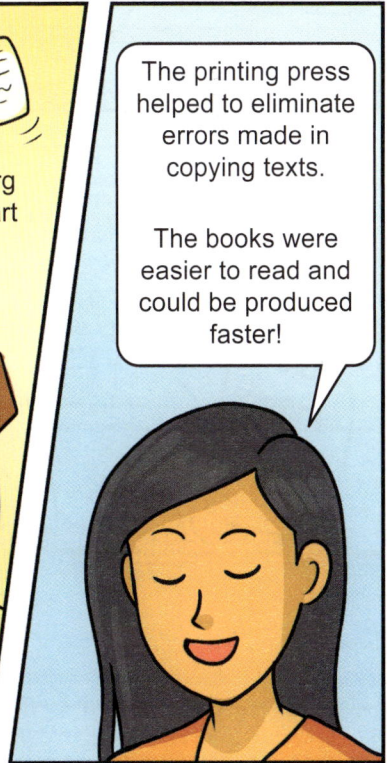

He Booked Us

What an amazing story!

Indeed! We can learn so much from him, such as working hard and being focused to achieve our dream...

Then seeing the results of our success! Do you know how important Johannes' invention was?

Uhhh...it managed to keep kids at home, studying every day?

Hahaha that's true! But seriously...

...the availability of the printed book meant that common people finally had access to knowledge, and information. No longer did those things belong to the rich and powerful only.

Knowledge

Information

Yes, it changed the way that many people lived. The commoners who wanted to improve themselves could now do so!

He Booked Us

Sounds like it made the world a fairer and better place!

Thanks for a wonderful story, Mum and Dad! I appreciate books much more now.

So...no more iPad bedtime stories?

JOHANNES GUTENBERG

Yes! Only stories from printed books for me!

The Gutenberg Bible

One of Johannes Gutenberg's major works was the Gutenberg Bible. It was the first printed version of the Bible and was considered a masterpiece for its high aesthetic and technical quality. It was also easy to read with 42 evenly spaced lines per page.

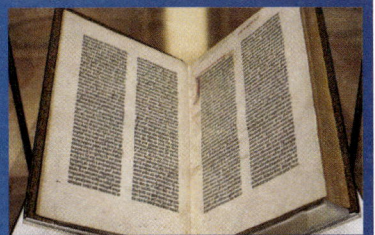

The Press Did Not Stop There

Johannes Gutenberg is considered one of the most influential people in human history because the printing press that he invented had many far-reaching effects!

The European Renaissance of the 15th and 16th centuries

This was a turning point in European history, where Europe is considered to have transited from the Middle Ages to modernity. The printing press made this possible through:

(i)   *The introduction of a modern banking and accounting system*
(ii) *Artistic development, with Leonardo da Vinci and Michelangelo inspiring the "Renaissance man" — a person knowledgeable in many different areas*

Leonardo da Vinci

The Scientific Revolution
Modern Science was introduced in this period, fuelled by developments in Astronomy, Mathematics, Physics, Biology and Chemistry. Many new ideas helped to transform society's view on nature. Some key publications that led to these groundbreaking ideas were:
(i)   De revolutionibus orbium coelestium (On the Revolutions of the Heavenly Spheres) *by Nicolaus Copernicus in 1543*
(ii) Principia *(which formulated the laws of motion and universal gravitation) by Isaac Newton in 1687*

Title page of *De revolutionibus orbium coelestium*

The Reformation

The Protestant Reformation that swept through Europe in the 1500s was also made possible by the printing press. Martin Luther's Ninety-five Theses *was printed and circulated widely, fueling the Reformation movement. Martin Luther later issued broadsheets to outline his anti-indulgences position and these broadsheets led to the development of the newspaper.*

Reproduction of the *Ninety-five Theses*

He Booked Us

The First Ever Video Gamer

Aaaarrrgghhhh, why do we keep losing?

Yes, we need help!

Wait, I know! Dad!!!

Is his dad good at video games?

RESTART?

Dad, you said you knew how we could be the first at video games. How? Please help!

Ha ha, you misheard me. I said I know who the FIRST video gamer was!

Hang on, there might be something there. If this guy was the very first video gamer, he SHOULD be good at it!

It's possible! Well, his name is Ralph Henry Baer.

Baer was born in 1922, in Pirmasens, Germany.

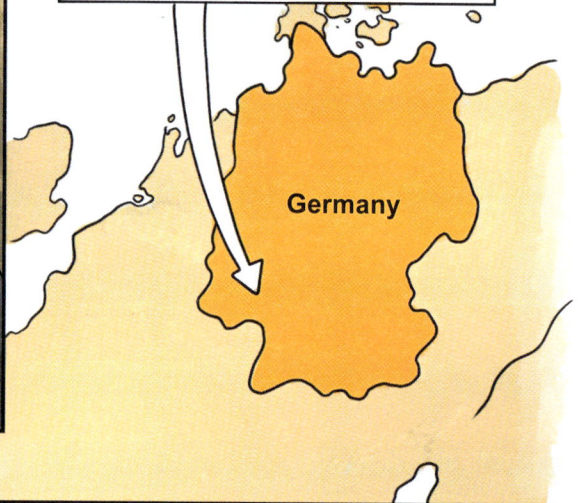

Germany

His childhood wasn't easy as his Jewish family received a lot of persecution when Adolf Hitler came to power.

When he was 14, Baer was expelled from his school.

You will be transferred to an all-Jewish school instead.

The First Ever Video Gamer

I'm worried that we will receive further persecution if we stay in Germany.

You're right.

Baer's family moved to New York City, USA, in 1938 and he became an American.

In his early days in the USA, Baer worked in a factory.

On the way to work one day, he saw an advertisement for a course in radio electronics.

That sounds interesting!

Radio!

NEWS

Baer quit his job and enrolled in the course. He completed it in 1940 and found a job as a radio service technician.

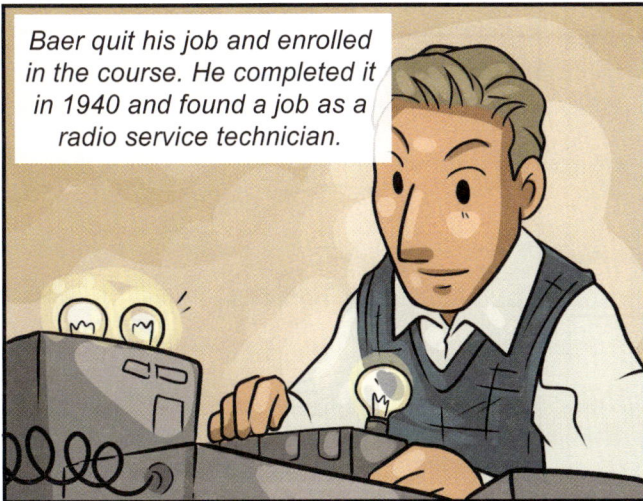

In 1951, while working for an electronics company named Loral...

Instead of using a television to watch boring programmes, why not use it to play simple games?

He approached some executives with his ideas.

So, no one was interested in the idea at all?

What a waste! They could have been playing video games much earlier!

I've an idea — how about offering games on television sets?

Huh? Who needs those?

In 1966, when he was working at Sanders Associates…

I believe my idea of having games on televisions still works!

Baer put together a 4-page proposal with his ideas.

More families can afford televisions! There is potential for a product that allows families to interact with their televisions!

Finally, Baer received some support.

We can give you US$2,500 and two engineers to help you!

Thank you!

Baer's team developed the "Brown Box", which was finally patented much later.

This console allowed people to play games such as football and tennis!

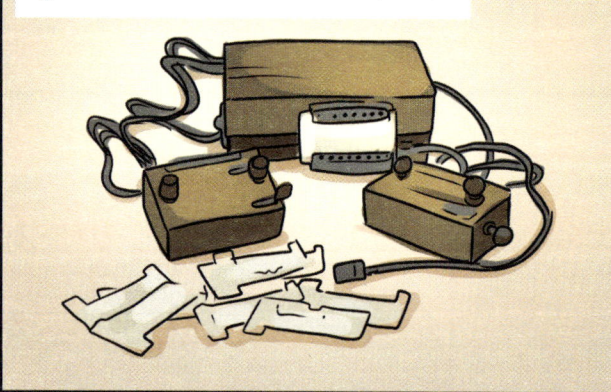

The First Ever Video Gamer

Intriguing Product

When Baer and his team brought their Brown Box for patenting, everyone in the building was excited about this new product. Within 15 minutes, every examiner on the floor of that building was in that office wanting to play the game.

And why was it called the "Brown Box"?

Maybe BROWN is the acronym for their new product! Better Racing On Winning Network?

Ha ha, good one! But it was named simply because of the brown tape used to make it look like wood!

Wow, that's a very simple name for a groundbreaking invention!

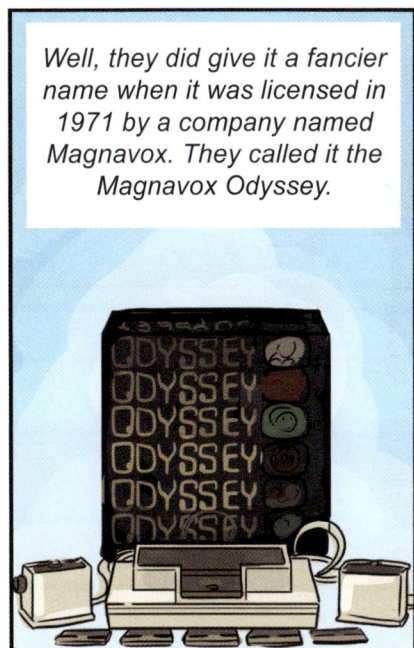

Well, they did give it a fancier name when it was licensed in 1971 by a company named Magnavox. They called it the Magnavox Odyssey.

Ahhhh yes, that sounds a lot more futuristic and cool!

Yes, what a wonderful story! I had no idea that was how the video game came about.

Wow! I am so inspired to invent something now!

That's great, but do remember that it is not easy. Ralph Baer had to overcome quite a few obstacles.

But he finally brought us this amazing machine, which has brought so much fun to so many people.

Yes! Let's get started inventing! We'll come up with a...

A BLACK BOX!

No, wait!!! That name has been taken already!

The First Ever Video Gamer

Not Brown but Black

The Black Box is a flight data recorder, which captures all the flight information in a specific way, so that authorities can retrieve this information when necessary, such as during an accident. Interestingly, "Black Boxes" are usually orange in colour.

FLIGHT RECORDER DO NOT OPEN

The Honours Inventor

Ralph Henry Baer truly enjoyed inventing. Even though he was more widely known as "The Father of Video Games", he invented a whole lot more and had over 150 patents to his name. In 2004, Ralph Baer was awarded the National Medal of Technology and Innovation by the US President in honour of his "groundbreaking and pioneering creation, development and commercialisation of interactive video games". In 2010, he was inducted into the National Inventors Hall of Fame in a ceremony held at Washington DC.

The National Medal of Technology

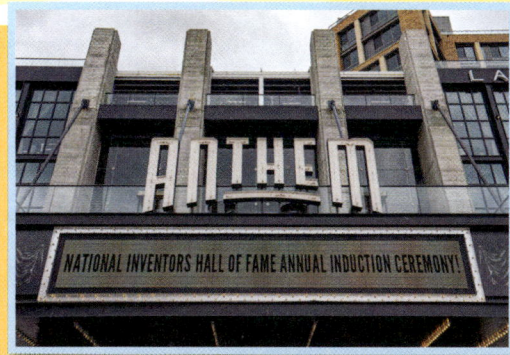

Venue of The National Inventors Hall of Fame Induction Ceremony

The Game of Invention

Among his many inventions, Ralph Baer was known mainly for those related to games, especially the following three:

(i) Simon – developed in 1978, along with Howard J. Morrison. This was a short-term memory skill game that was extremely popular till the late 1990s.

(ii) Super Simon – developed in 1979 for game company Milton Bradley. This sequel to Simon was another electronic pattern-matching game that was immensely popular as well.

(iii) Maniac – developed in 1979 for the Ideal Toy Company. Harder to play than Simon, this game tests players' ability to handle changes in sounds and lights.

Simon

Super Simon

Maniac

Customising Cancer Treatment

During dinner one evening...

So how was your sleepover at your cousins' place? Did you eat well?

It was fun! And yes, Aunt June and Uncle Steven were feeding us plenty of food!

Yes, and Uncle Steven was so funny! He kept getting mixed up.

Oh no, did he forget that you are allergic to shellfish and that your sister cannot take mangoes?

No no, he remembered that. But he kept thinking that Oli likes chicken and I like fish, when it's the other way round!

Yes, he kept piling my plate with chicken and Jay's plate with fish!

Oh, my dear brother! He doesn't have a good memory. Did you tell him?

No, we didn't want to embarrass him, so we secretly exchanged our food each time.

That reminds me of what I read about Dr Dean Ho, who is doing something like that, but in medicine.

What? He exchanged patients' medicines secretly?

Ha ha, thank goodness, no! But he did give them what they needed.

What do you mean, Dad? Don't we always get the medicines that we need from doctors?

That's true, but where cancer treatment is concerned, they realised that different patients required different amounts of medication, depending on the nature and severity of their illness.

Cancer
Cancer is a disease where abnormal cells in the body divide rapidly and uncontrollably. These cells usually develop into a lump known as a tumour and may spread to other parts of the body. If untreated, cancer may be life-threatening.

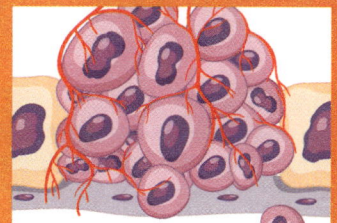

Oh, I know that treatment for cancer patients is called chemotherapy!

That's right! Patients used to be given standard doses of chemotherapy drugs.

But doctors began to realise that some patients don't need so much, while others need a bit more.

So, what did Dr Ho do?

He and his team did research on nanomedicine using nanodiamonds. This enables them to give each cancer patient just the right amount of medication they need.

'Nano' refers to something extremely small! Nanodiamonds must be tiny!

That's right. They found out that these tiny diamonds are also very suitable for killing bacteria and mould, due to factors such as their size and shape.

NANOMEDICINE

Dean and Team

Dr Dean Ho made many important discoveries in nanomedicine with his team at the Department of Biomedical Engineering, National University of Singapore. They pioneered the nanodiamond platforms for cancer therapy, healing of wounds and other areas as well.

So, these nanodiamonds are able to reach the exact spots where they are needed, such as the cancerous cells of the body, instead of being distributed all around. Effectiveness multiplied!

That's right! Dr Ho and his team have certainly contributed greatly to the field of medicine with their work and discoveries.

Well, maybe Dr Ho can advise Uncle Steven on how to give others what they need exactly.

More May NOT be Better

With chemotherapy, it has been traditionally considered that as much medication as can be tolerated by the patient should be given to destroy the maximum number of cancer cells. However, recent studies have revealed that using targeted amounts may be more efficient. This also reduces unseen toxicity of medication as well as the associated high financial costs.

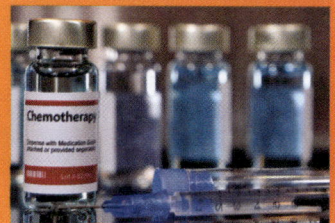

Life and Lessons of Dr Dean Ho

Dr Dean Ho grew up in Los Angeles, USA, because his parents had migrated there for their further studies. It was there where he was ingrained with the idea that success meant adding value to society with his achievements. This helped him to embark on research to find more suitable medication and dosages for patients, especially those suffering from cancer.

Customising Cancer Treatment

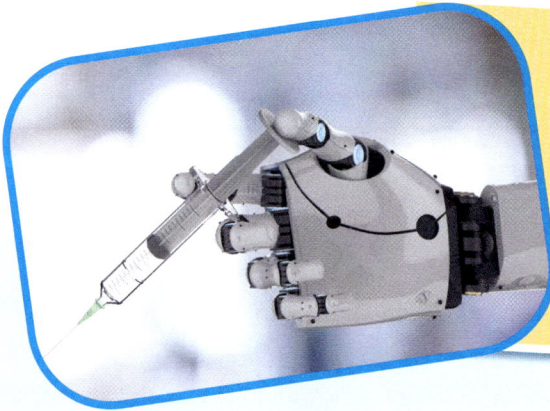

Dr Ho collaborated with his father to optimise drug therapy for liver transplant patients, to help prevent organ rejection. They used Artificial Intelligence to recommend a suitable medicine dosage for these patients. They were greatly encouraged to see them being discharged more promptly from intensive care, some as much as one month earlier.

After moving to Singapore, Dr Ho and his team at NUS (National University of Singapore) started research on nanomedicine. They used nanoscopic diamonds to carry medication to specific cells in the body that have been infected with a particular disease. This allowed a more targeted approach that not only reduced the cost of therapy, but also increased the efficiency of the medication. It was a win-win solution that could lead to many other wonderful possibilities in the field of medicine.

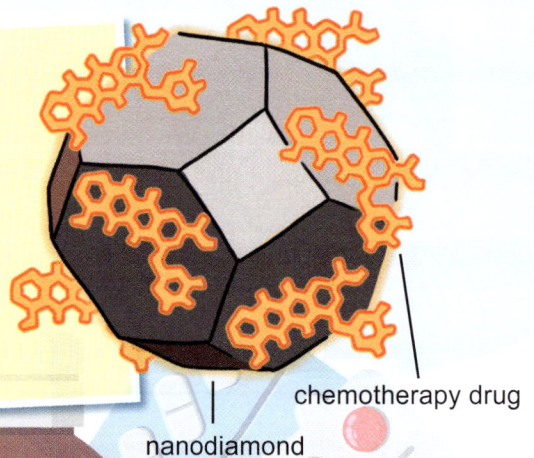

chemotherapy drug

nanodiamond

Carbon Conqueror

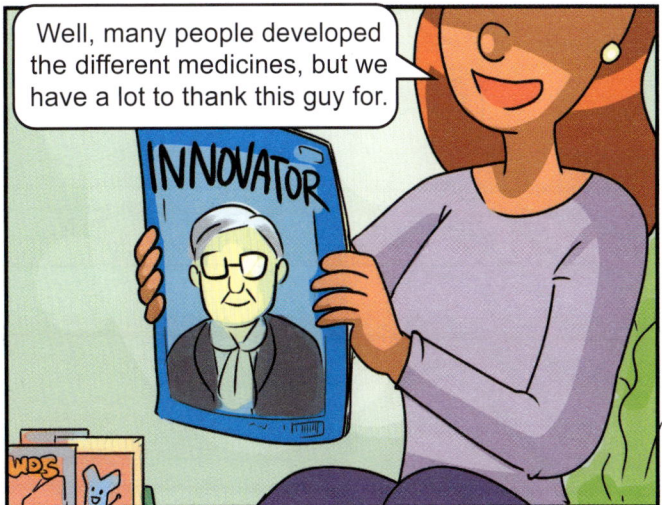

DOSE OF THE RIGHT MEDICINE

Panel 1: Is he the one who is going to give me the medicine?

Panel 2: Farmer? What did he plant?

Panel 3: P-h-a-r-m-a, sis! Pharmaceutics refers to the study and production of medicines.

Panel 4: Ha ha, no. This man is Mr Ei-ichi Negishi, someone who made big contributions in the field of pharmaceutics.

Panel 5: That's right. And Negishi discovered something that helped greatly in the production of medicines.

Panel 6: What did he discover? Was it a secret antidote to some deadly disease?

Panel 7: Ha ha, no! But he was the one who discovered a way to harness carbon molecules.

Constant Mover

Ei-chi Negishi was born in Hsinking, the capital of Manchukuo, in July 1935. Following the transfer of his father who worked at the South Manchuria Railway in 1936, he moved to Harbin. In 1943, when he was nine, the Negishi family moved to Incheon, and a year later to Kyongsong Prefecture (now Seoul). In November 1945, three months after World War II ended, they moved to Japan.

200F

Carbon Conqueror

26

Negishi came up with a technique to make carbon atoms combine with others to form new compounds. He likened this process to stacking Lego bricks.

How does that help us?

This process has helped in the production of medicines such as antibiotics and drugs for asthma!

I see. He must have worked very hard!

Yes, he was passionate about Chemistry and helping others.

Beyond that, I feel that he had a wise approach to life.

How so, Mum?

Negishi felt that there were four ingredients for happiness.

Four? What are they?

First, good health. Second, a happy family – make that a priority.

Then the third ingredient is a good job.

Yes, a high-paying one!

Shining Student

Due to his excellence in studies, Ei-ichi Negishi was admitted to an elite secondary school a year ahead of what would have been his graduation from grammar school. He got into the University of Tokyo at the young age of 17. Later, he earned a Fulbright Scholarship, helping him obtain a PhD from the University of Pennsylvania in 1963.

The Sharing Scientist

Negishi's character was outstanding too! He did not patent his groundbreaking findings because he wanted other scientists to be able to freely use the research. It was a very generous move compared to how other scientists tend to protect their research.

The Negishi Reaction

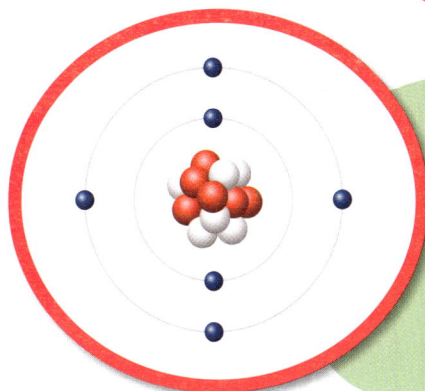

Electronic structure
of a carbon atom

In order to create complex molecules for medicines, the knitting of carbon atoms is very important. This was hard to achieve as carbon atoms are very stable and do not readily react. Past attempts at getting them to react have led to unwanted by-products.

In 1977, after much experimentation, Ei-ichi Negishi managed to use a zinc atom to transfer a carbon atom to a palladium atom. The carbon atom then joined another carbon atom to form a new molecule. In this way, he could form a great variety of molecules in a way that saves a lot of money and energy. This method was known as the Negishi Coupling Reaction.

This discovery is extremely important in the field of pharmaceutics, as it led to the production of many more medicines that were previously not attainable. It is estimated that about a quarter of all reactions in the pharmaceutical industry use this technique today.

Carbon Conquerors

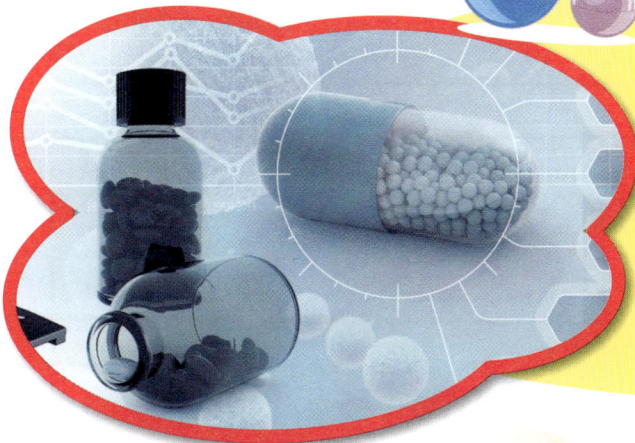

Mr MRI

What's wrong, Emma? You seem troubled.

It's my Grandpa, Ms Wie. He's feeling a lot of pain in his stomach and the doctors want him to do an MRI. But he is afraid and doesn't want to go.

Do you know why he is afraid of doing an MRI?

Yes, his friends have told him that taking an MRI scan is a very scary procedure.

I see…maybe you can tell your Grandpa about Sir Peter Mansfield! Hang on, let me find a photo…

Here!

Huh? Who is he? He looks like a doctor.

Well, not really. He's actually a physicist and an inventor.

Oh! Did he invent the MRI machine?

No, the inventor of the MRI is Raymond Damadian. But Sir Peter Mansfield made the MRI so much better and easier to use!

Oh, what does the MRI do anyway?

Well, MRI stands for Magnetic Resonance Imaging. It is a method of scanning our bodies so that we can see what may be causing harm in our bodies.

But why would anyone find it scary?

It could be the weird noises and lights that appear during an MRI.

So, Grandpa and his friends are just afraid of some noises and lights?

Ha ha! I think the strapping in also makes it quite daunting. You are not supposed to move during an MRI scan.

Raymond Damadian
Raymond Vahan Damadian was an American physician who first proposed the Magnetic Resonance body scan in 1969. He then performed the first full-body scan of a human being in 1977.

31

Mr MRI

Hmmm….being strapped in, hearing weird sounds and seeing strange lights…sounds familiar.

I know! I'll just ask Grandpa to imagine he is taking a roller coaster ride!

Yes, I guess you can try that, especially if your Grandpa likes roller coaster rides. But there are other reasons an MRI scan can be scary.

For example, being exposed to these strong magnetic waves for a long time isn't good for the body.

Oh dear…

It could also cause the body to heat up, leading to other complications.

Heat up??

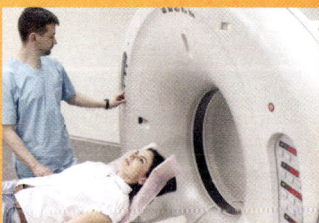

Weird Noises During an MRI

If you are wondering where the noises during an MRI scan come from, they are actually caused by the metal coils in the MRI machine! When these coils receive electrical pulses, they vibrate when generating a magnetic field. This strong vibration of the coils produces the loud noises.

Not THAT hot. But still, it's not good for our body. That's why we have to thank Sir Peter Mansfield for his inventions regarding the MRI!

What did he do?

First of all, Sir Mansfield discovered "slice imaging".

That sounds painful!

It's not! It allows us to scan specific parts of the body, allowing us to zoom in on an area.

That should give us clearer pictures!

0 200 400 600 800 1000

Multiple Slice Imaging

Exactly! In the course of his work, Mansfield became his own guinea pig — he was the first person to have his abdomen scanned using this technique!

That's not all! He also came up with Echo-planar imaging, or EPI.

Wow!

The EPI technique allowed him to capture rapidly changing processes, such as a beating heart or blood flow.

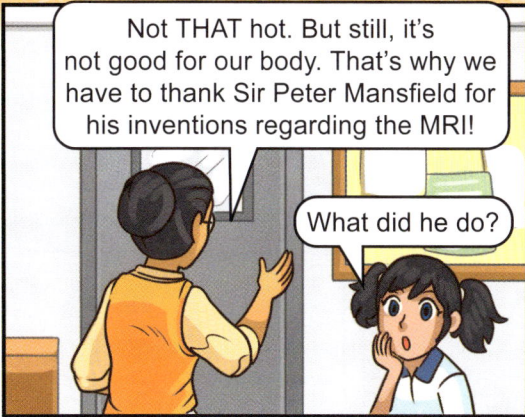

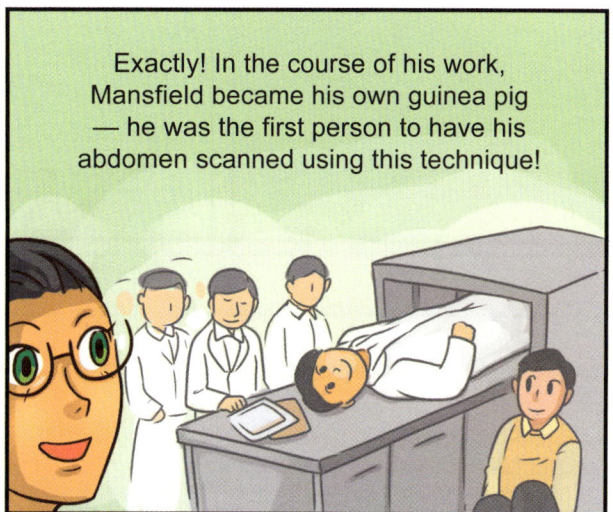

Exploring the EPI

Echo-planar imaging (EPI) allows us to acquire a Magnetic Resonance (MR) image in less than a second! There are single-shot and multi-shot echo-planar images, with the latter providing much clearer, high-quality images. EPI can now be applied to many parts of the body, including the heart, abdomen and brain.

33

Mr MRI

That's amazing!

It really improved diagnostics in many diseases.

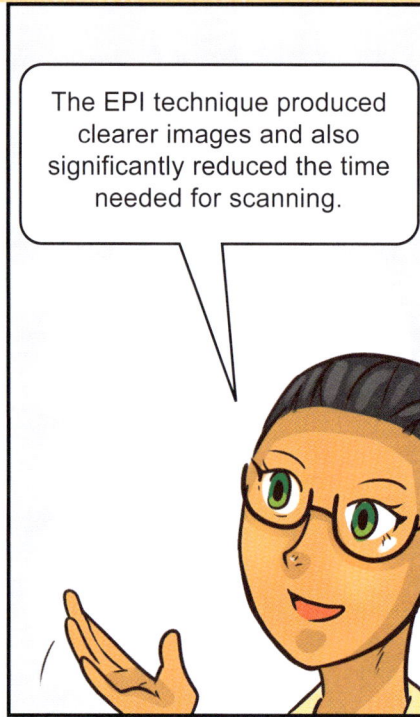

The EPI technique produced clearer images and also significantly reduced the time needed for scanning.

Less time for Grandpa on the "roller coaster" then!

What's important is that the MRI is one step closer to getting an accurate diagnosis. It will help his doctors decide on the best way to treat him.

Thanks for this fantastic information, Ms Wie! I'll tell Grandpa everything you said!

One week later…

Ms Wie! Guess what? I managed to persuade Grandpa to go for his MRI scan, with the information you gave me!

That's great! I hope he enjoyed his "roller coaster ride".

Yes, it turns out that he really likes roller coasters! But he was most happy when the doctors told him there's no tumour in his stomach!

That's wonderful! I'm so happy for you and your Grandpa.

Yes, and I must thank you, as well as Sir Peter Mansfield!

The Life of Sir Peter Mansfield

1933

On 9 Oct 1933, Peter Mansfield was born in Lambeth, London. He was the youngest of three sons.

Lambeth, London

At the age of 15, a careers teacher told him that Science was not suitable for him. Soon after, he left school and worked as a printer's assistant.

1948

When he was 18, Mansfield developed an interest in rocketry and worked at the Rocket Propulsion Department of the Ministry of Supply in Wescott, Buckinghamshire.

1951

1959

In 1959, he graduated with a degree in Physics and in 1962, received his PhD. Two years later, he became a lecturer at Nottingham University while continuing his research in MRI.

1962

1993

Peter Mansfield was knighted in 1993 and ten years later, received the Nobel Prize in Physiology or Medicine.

2003

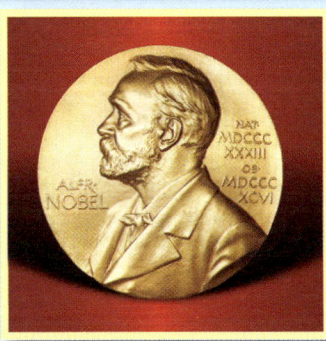

The Nobel Prize

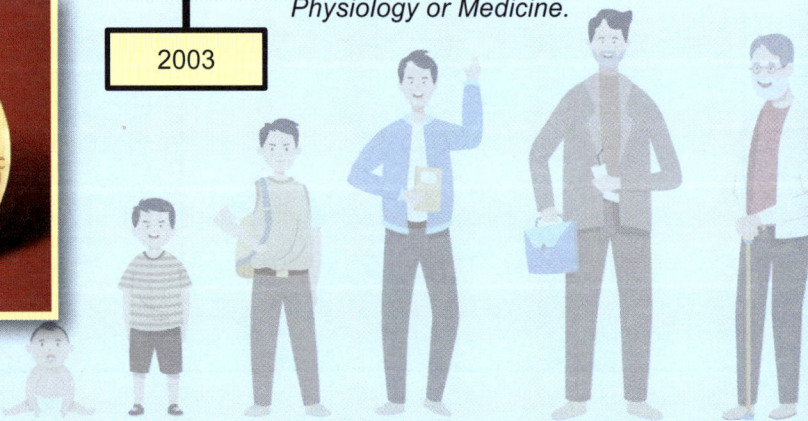

36

Mr MRI

Heavyweight in Light Transmission

Heavyweight in Light Transmission

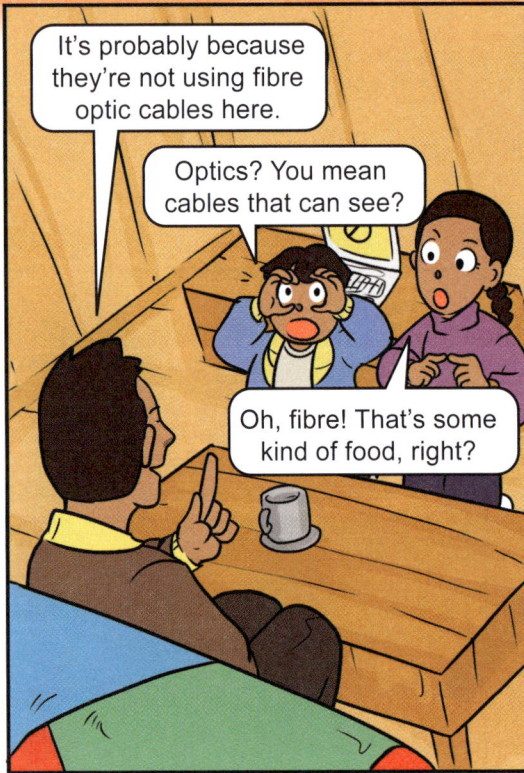

It's probably because they're not using fibre optic cables here.

Optics? You mean cables that can see?

Oh, fibre! That's some kind of food, right?

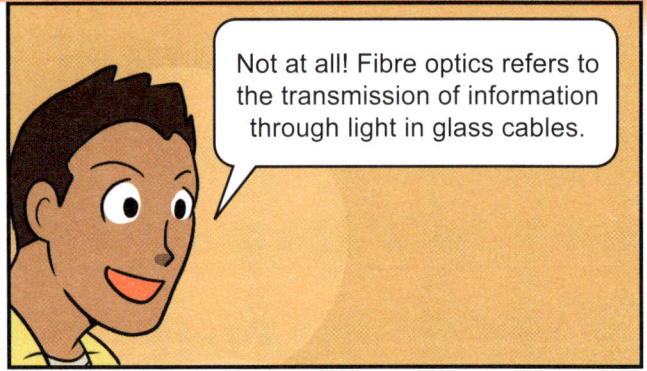

Not at all! Fibre optics refers to the transmission of information through light in glass cables.

But I don't see any glass cables at our house. Do we use them too?

Of course we do! but they are usually hidden underground or within the walls.

Wow, these fibre optic cables really make a big difference in our lives.

That's right! And since we don't have much connectivity here, let's find out more about the guy who brought us fibre optics.

Might as well! Charles Kao. Hey, he has the same birthday as me – November 4!

But he's born in 1933, 80 years before you!

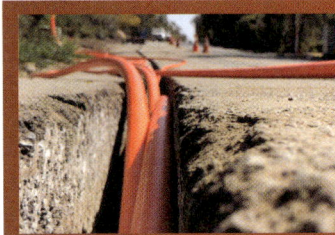

Where are those Fibre Optic Cables?

Fibre optic cables may be installed underground or above ground, on poles. Most places prefer to lay them underground, even though this method costs more. They are kept safe from various forms of damage when buried underground. There are fibre optic cables under the sea too!

Hi, I'm Charles Kao! I was born in Shanghai, but my family moved to Hong Kong when I was 15.

Later, I grew up in Taiwan before moving to London to study engineering. I was always moving! Maybe that's why I wanted to find ways to move information faster!

People call me the "godfather of broadband" because I helped to discover broadband. It was a pretty tough process.

My team and I did much research and discovered that glass fibres could be used for long-distance information transfer.

We proposed that this would be way more effective than the copper wires used at that time.

In early 1966, brimming with confidence, we brought our findings and proposal to one of the biggest telecommunication companies then – Bell Labs…

39

Heavyweight in Light Transmission

But the idea was too radical for them at that time, and we were rejected.

Devastated but undeterred, we decided to bring our findings to Japan…

Interestingly, we received some support there!

As a result, we were able to visit glass and polymer factories, where we discussed methods of glass fibre manufacturing with engineers, scientists and even businessmen.

In the process, we learnt so much! One of the most important lessons was that the amount of signal loss was affected by the purity of the glass being used.

We poured these findings into our research and were able to show even more positive results. This led to Bell Labs becoming interested in our work in 1969.

That's when Bell Labs began to pour much time and money into our research and development of fibre optics, which is now being used all over the world.

If there is one thing I have learnt, it is to never give up. You can one day turn your doubters into believers and supporters.

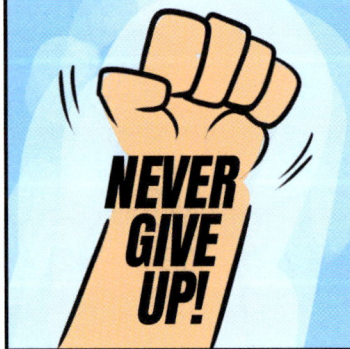

1969

NEVER GIVE UP!

Heavyweight in Light Transmission

The World of Fibre Optics

Before the era of fibre optic cables, copper wires were used to transmit information. They could carry signals for about 100 metres, while fibre optic cables can transmit for about 40 kilometres! Another major advantage of fibre optics can be found in the amount of signal loss. In 100 metres, about 90% of the signal is lost in copper cables, but for fibre optic cables, it is only about 3%.

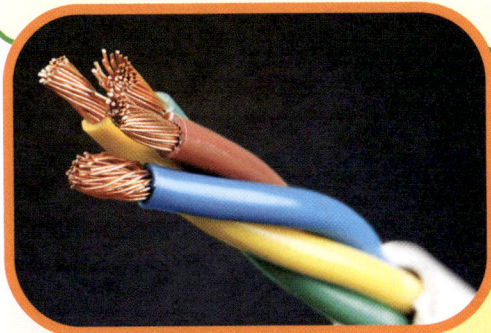

Copper cables versus fibre optic cables

We may not realise it, but fibre optics is all around us today. Here are some examples of things that make use of fibre optics!

41

1. Communication

2. The Internet

3. Computer Networking

4. Fairy lights

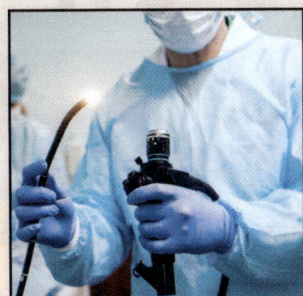

5. Medical equipment such as endoscopes

6. Cable TV

Heavyweight in Light Transmission

Pioneer Programmer

EEEEE—

This is so cool, Mum! How do they teach the robots to do this?

They have programmed the robots to follow instructions. Remember the programming course you attended last month?

Oh yes! That was when I learnt to programme a game!

Do you mean the one with a stickman moving around in circles? I wouldn't call that a game!

I thought that was a good first attempt. We all have to start somewhere!

Exactly. Programming isn't an easy subject to learn.

But Mum, I heard it's much easier now. Is that true? Was it really tough learning to programme in the past?

You're right, Jeannie! In the past, computer programmes were written entirely with symbols!

But I used mainly words to write my stickman game!

Well, you have Grace Hopper to thank for that.

Who's that?

Is she a great programming teacher?

43

Pioneer Programmer

Old is Gold?

Here are some old programming languages (and the years they were created) that are still in use today:

Fortran – 1957   Lisp – 1958
C – 1972   SQL – 1974
Ada – 1977-1983

Pioneer Programmer

Better than that! She helped to invent one of the most common programming languages used today.

Ah yes, the programming that our teacher told us about! It's called COOLBOY or something…

Hahaha! Close enough! It's really COBOL, and it stands for COmmon Business Oriented Language.

Did all of the older programming languages use symbols only? That must have been tough!

It must have been! But Grace Hopper believed that a programming language based on English was possible. So, she worked very hard to produce one.

COBOL
COmmon Business-Oriented Language

First time in English!

In 1954, Grace Hopper created the FLOW-MATIC programming language, which was based on English. It was later extended to create COBOL, a high-level programming language which is still widely used today.

So, she was one of the people behind COBOL!

Yes, in fact, some people affectionately call her Grandma COBOL.

That is so cute, Mum. I wonder what kind of person she was.

Well, one of her most outstanding traits was her curiosity…

When Grace Hopper was 7 years old…

I wonder how this works?

Mother, may I have another clock?

Pioneer Programmer

Grace, what are you doing?

From now on, you're only allowed one clock!

I was trying to find out how the clock works!

In 1941, during World War II, Pearl Harbour was attacked.

I'm going to join the Navy and be part of the war effort!

Hopper's application was rejected because she was 34 and considered too old. She was also underweight.

It's alright. I'll just have to try again!

Wow, how underweight was she?

Well, the Navy's minimum weight requirement was 54 kg and she was about 7 kg less than that!

Hopper didn't give up and tried again. Finally, in December 1943…

Hooray! I've been allowed to join the Navy WAVES or the Women Accepted for Voluntary Emergency Service!

Wow, it's great that she never gave up!

Tell us more about her, Mum.

Mathematician in the Navy

Grace Hopper was a mathematics professor at Vassar College when she obtained a leave of absence to join the Navy WAVES (Women Accepted for Voluntary Emergency Service). She trained at the Naval Reserve Midshipmen's School and graduated first in her class. She was then assigned to the Bureau of Ships Computation Project at Harvard University, where she served on the Mark I computer programming staff.

Pioneer Programmer

Grace Hopper continued to work on computers. That's when she invented the first computer compiler and subsequently the FLOW-MATIC computer language. Throughout her career, she remained as a Navy Reserve Officer.

I guess she really wanted to serve her country!

And serve she did! At 60 years old, she was recalled to help standardise the Navy's multiple computer languages.

It's like she never retired!

She did, at 79 years old! She was a rear admiral by then, and the oldest serving officer in the U.S. Armed Forces.

Me too! And I want to develop a better game than my stickman one.

That is so inspiring, Mum. I want to be like Grace Hopper.

That's great! Well, you already know some important qualities to succeed as a great programmer.

Curiosity!

Perseverance!

NEVER GIVE UP!

Hahaha yes! But in the meantime, let's enjoy the food that this programme has brought us.

47

Language of Change

When Grace Hopper first proposed developing a programming language that used English words only, she did not receive much support. Among other things, she was told that…

Computers don't understand English!

Computers can only do arithmetic!

But Grace did not give up as she felt strongly that...

It's much easier for most people to write an English statement than it is to use symbols.

Her idea was not accepted for three years but she continued working on the programme known as "A Compiler". It was finally ready in 1952 and what it did was to "translate mathematical notation into machine code".

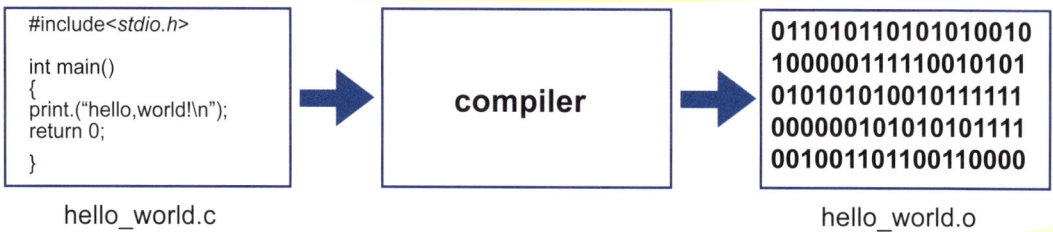

```
#include<stdio.h>

int main()
{
print.("hello,world!\n");
return 0;

}
```

hello_world.c

compiler

```
0110101101010100 10
1000001111100101 01
0101010100101111 11
0000001010101011 11
0010011011001100 00
```

hello_world.o

This evolved into COBOL which was extremely useful for data processing and is still the major computer language used today.

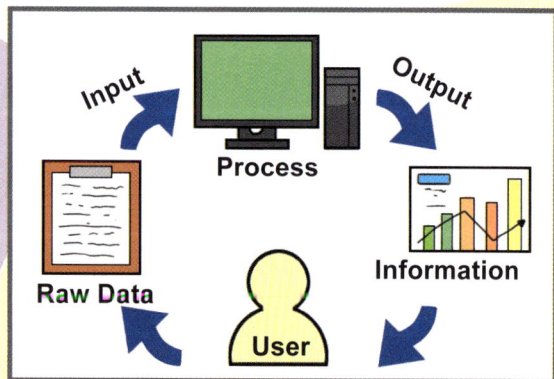

Input

Output

Process

Information

Raw Data

User

Data processing

Solar Superhero

I think this is turning out to be a bad idea. The heat is killing me.

Yes, we started out with burning enthusiasm, but now, we're just burning… with angst!

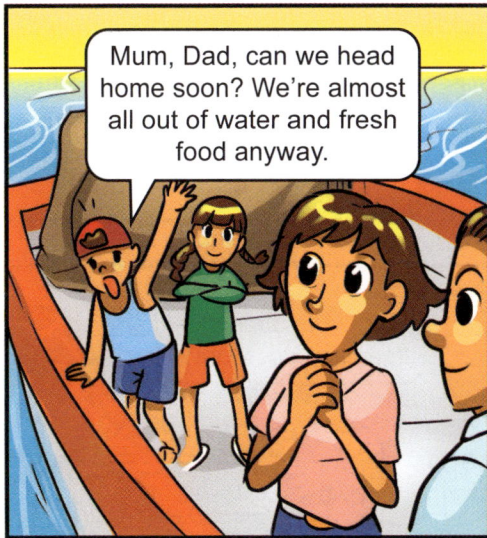

Mum, Dad, can we head home soon? We're almost all out of water and fresh food anyway.

I guess now's the time for us to bring out our secret weapons?

Sure!

Glen and Winnie, let us introduce you to…Maria Telkes!!!

Wait, who is Maria Telkes?

She's the one who invented these amazing devices!

Indeed! This one is a solar-powered water desalination machine.

I've heard of desalination machines! They help us turn seawater to drinkable water, right?

During World War II, downed American soldiers who were stranded in the Pacific Ocean had no access to drinking water. Maria Telkes's solar-powered desalination device saved their lives!

Wow, that sounds really cool! Can we try it?

And what does this machine do, Mum?

Solar Superhero

Reverse osmosis

External pressure

Fresh water

Seawater

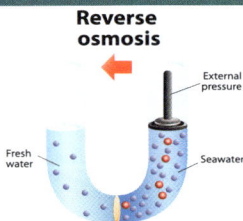

How Desalination Machines Work

The main idea is to force water from the ocean through tightly wrapped, semipermeable membranes under high pressure. The membranes allow only the smaller water molecules to pass through, leaving salt and other impurities behind.

This is a solar-powered oven, Winnie. Also perfect for sweltering weather like this.

You mean, we can cook with energy from the sun? No need for charcoal or gas?

That's right! Solar energy from the sun can enter the box directly or get reflected in. The insulator at the bottom allows the box to retain heat and cook food!

It's such a useful device!

Definitely! The temperature in Maria Telkes' oven could go up to 350°C, enough to bake bread or roast food!

That's amazing. I can't wait to get started!

Sure!

51

Solar Superhero

Hot and Sunny Food

Around 1953, Maria Telkes decided to work on solar energy research at the New York City College of Engineering. It was there where she developed the solar-powered oven, helping people who lack the technology to heat their food with the sun's energy. It was useful in remote areas of tribal India and similar ones are still being used widely today.

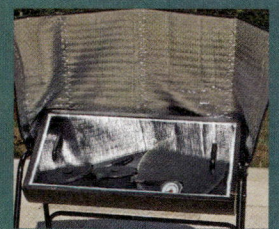

Solar Superhero

This is so cool, Dad! I am so glad it's so hot today!

Yes, knowing that the food was cooked by the sun makes it taste especially good!

Well, we have Maria Telkes to thank for these amazing machines!

She worked on many other things, such as solar dryers, solar thermoelectric systems for use in outer space…even the first fully solar-powered home!

Yes, her inventions have definitely brought much comfort and relief to many people!

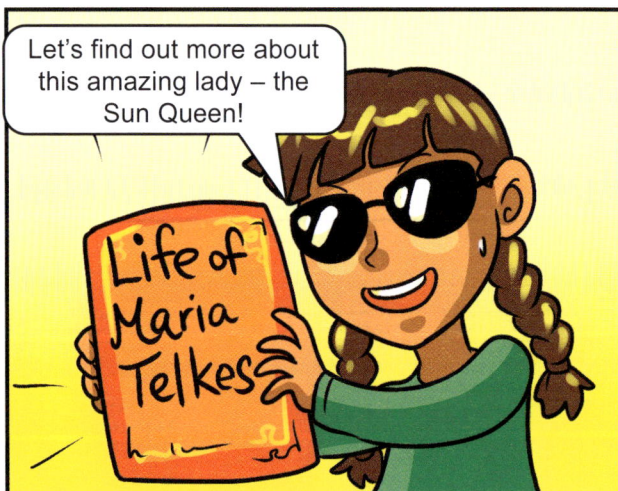

Let's find out more about this amazing lady – the Sun Queen!

Life of Maria Telkes

The Sun Queen

Maria Telkes was born in Budapest, Hungary, in the year 1900. She received her education in Budapest, right up to her days at the University of Budapest, where she graduated with a degree in Physical Chemistry in 1920, and a PhD in 1924.

After that, she moved to the United States and worked at the Cleveland Clinic Foundation, investigating the energy that living organisms produce. Maria also worked at Westinghouse and the prestigious Massachusetts Institute of Technology (MIT).

Massachusetts Institute of Technology (MIT)

Other than her solar-powered desalination machine and solar-powered oven, Maria was also deeply interested in developing solar-powered homes. Her Dover Sun House project in 1948 was not considered a success when some of its components started failing after a few years of usage. However, in 1972, she helped to build the first house to generate both heat and electricity from the sun. Then in 1981, she helped the US Department of Energy to build the first fully solar-powered home in Massachusetts.

A house with solar panels

53

Solar Superhero

Soil Saviour

Joyce, Sandy and Mabel are taking a break from their training.

Sandy, are you alright? You seem to be slower than usual today.

She's just giving us a chance to catch up to her. She's usually so far ahead!

No way! Truth is, I've been feeling some pain in my knee recently.

Oh dear, are you ok? Maybe you should stop running for some time.

But our competition is coming up soon!

Or maybe you should do what George Washington Carver did.

Who's that?

And what did he do?

George Carver was an agricultural scientist who was famous for promoting crop rotation in order to save the soil.

How does rotating crops save the soil? I can only see it killing the crops.

CRACK

Rotating crops, Sandy. Not twisting them.

I know what that means! It refers to regularly changing the type of crops being planted.

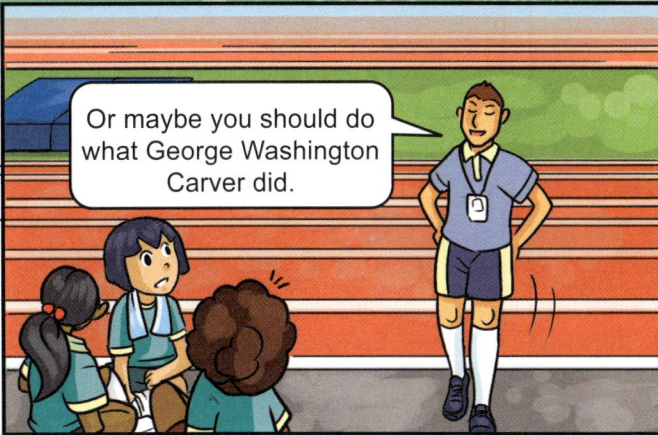

Crop Rotation

Crop rotation is widely practised all over the world today. Other than maintaining soil health, it is also an important strategy for dealing with diseases, weeds and pests.

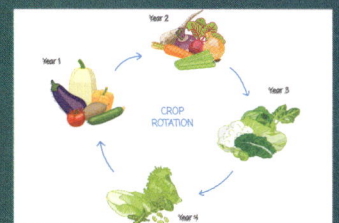

During George Carver's time, many farmers were destroying their farmlands by repeatedly planting cotton.

Why are we always planting cotton?

It's very popular! Many people want to buy cotton now.

This can't be good! Planting cotton removes a lot of nitrogen from the soil and damages it! Soon, we won't be able to grow anything else!

Please, try planting something else!

Such as?

Try growing sweet potatoes and peanuts. These crops will replenish the nitrogen in the soil and ultimately, improve your cotton yields!

It's worth a try…but what would we do with sweet potatoes and peanuts?

How do I encourage landowners to grow other crops?

Most Popular Fabric

Cotton is probably the most popular fabric in the world and there are reasons for it. It is easy to care for cotton, and it is comfortable in all types of weather. Even in hot and humid weather, cotton fibres absorb perspiration from the body and release it on the surface so that it evaporates.

I know! Maybe I can invent new and different uses for these crops!

Carver founded a research laboratory to develop hundreds of applications for these new crops, so that he could popularise them.

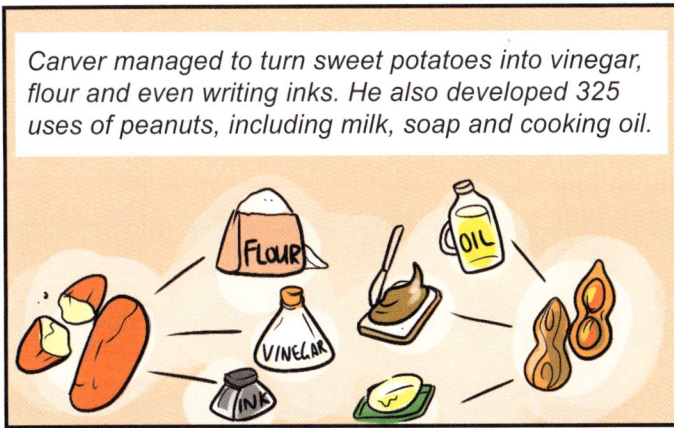

Carver managed to turn sweet potatoes into vinegar, flour and even writing inks. He also developed 325 uses of peanuts, including milk, soap and cooking oil.

FLOUR

OIL

VINEGAR

INK

That should really help! My parents are always asking me WHY I buy new things and WHAT I can use them for.

Haha mine too! So, Coach, it sounds like Mr George Carver was very successful in what he did.

Carver and his assistants promoted applications and recipes of these new crops, distributing this information in the form of agricultural bulletins.

A Mobile Classroom
Carver designed a mobile classroom to bring education out to the farmers. He taught them how and why they should rotate crops.

57

Soil Saviour

He certainly was. And he used that fame for a good cause too!

By donating huge amounts of money to charity?

He was probably a great philanthropist too, but Carver used his fame to go around giving talks on environmentalism and racial harmony.

Wow, he had everything going for him, didn't he?

Soil Saviour

Well, things were not always easy for him. As an African American at that time, he was on the receiving end of quite a lot of discrimination. In fact, he was born into slavery, which was not abolished yet.

Wow, and despite all the discrimination, he managed to accomplish so much? That is so impressive!

Discriminated But Not Downcast

As a young boy, the public school near Carver's home did not admit black students, so he travelled about 16 kilometres to another town to look for a school for black children. When he arrived at the town, the school was closed and he had to sleep in a barn near the school.

And inspirational too! Ok, Coach, I'll take your advice...or should I say...George Carver's advice?

That's great! In fact, all of you can try this out, to prevent injuries.

You want us to go plant peanuts and sweet potatoes, like George Carver?

Hahaha I don't think so! Coach probably wants us to do other sports instead of simply running all the time.

Exactly! Try to swim and maybe cycle, so that you rotate the use of your muscles and not wear them out.

Sure, Coach! We'll do it the George Carver way!

59

Soil Saviour

Death and Legacy

In his last years, Carver donated his life savings of almost US$60,000 to create the George Washington Carver Foundation. His birthplace in Missouri was established as a national monument.

Success of the Soil Saviour

Tuskegee University

George Washington Carver received his Master of Science degree in 1896. In that same year, he was invited to head the Agriculture Department of the Tuskegee Institute (now Tuskegee University). They paid him a salary that was above average and provided him with two rooms for his personal use, drawing jealousy from his colleagues.

Carver was well-respected as a botanist and a scientist. He wrote for a newspaper column called "Professor Carter's Advice" and provided free advice to business leaders who came to seek his help. He even met with three American presidents — Franklin Roosevelt, Calvin Coolidge and Theodore Roosevelt.

A postage stamp featuring George Washington Carver

A bust made in his honour at the George Washington Carver National Monument in Southern Missouri

Some of his other notable achievements include:
- Receiving the Spingarn Medal in 1923, awarded for outstanding achievement
- Receiving an honorary doctorate from Simpson College in 1928
- Receiving the Roosevelt Medal for outstanding contribution to southern agriculture in 1939
- Establishing the George Washington Carver Foundation in 1940 to fund agricultural research

The George Washington Carver Museum was officially recognised in 1938 at the Tuskegee Institute. This was done upon the request of President Frederick D. Patterson.

Soil Saviour

Clean, Green Scientist

Clean, Green Scientist

Factories like those will destroy all this beauty soon! It's all the fault of science and technology!

Uhhhh…that's not exactly true.

What do you mean, Simon? I agree with Theo here. Scientific progress has led to lots of pollution.

That's true, but… have you heard of Dr Pimchai Chaiyen?

Pimchai…who? Is she a campaigner against technology?

Not really. In fact, she's quite the opposite.

Polluted Air Everywhere

It is estimated that 90% of people in the world breathe air that contains a lot of pollutants. In South and East Asia, about 15% of deaths in the low-income countries are related to air pollution.

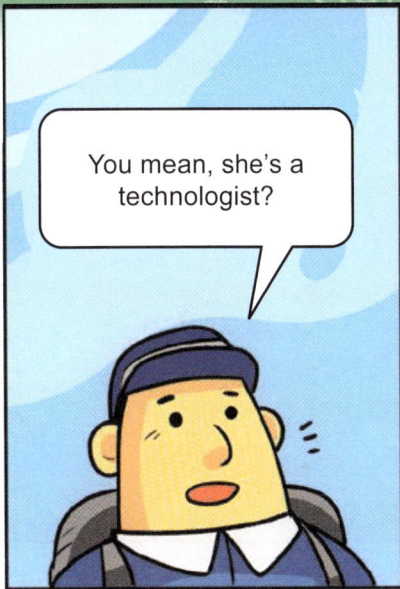

You mean, she's a technologist?

Yes, she's a scientist. BUT she strongly believes in caring for the environment through science and technology!

Is that even possible?

Yes, it is! Dr Chaiyen and her team research on ways to improve our environment. For example, they use biocatalysis.

63

They use…biological cats to conduct experiments?

Ha ha, no! Biocatalysis refers to the use of natural substances such as enzymes to speed up chemical reactions.

How does that benefit our environment?

By using these natural substances, less toxic materials and wastes are produced in these chemical processes.

Ah, yes! I learnt that these chemical wastes are one of the greatest contributors to global warming.

That's right! Dr Chaiyen and her team also work on Synthetic Biology!

That's another big term! Does it refer to a transforming kind of Biology?

Ha ha, I know where you got that from — Synthesis and Transformation!

Well, your guess is actually partially right!

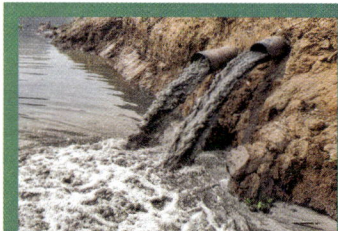

Clean, Green Scientist

Concern Over Chemicals

Chemical wastes can destroy the environment in many ways. One of the most common ways is when they get into streams, rivers and lakes. They are then carried to other areas and have toxic effects on animals and plants.

Synthetic Biology is a field of science that involves the creation or redesigning of organisms or systems that are already found in nature.

Transformers!!!

Ha ha, yes, these transformed products are meant for specific purposes, such as transforming "Trash to Treasure".

Wow, I'm starting to like this Dr Chaiyen already! She's doing some cool stuff!

Then this next technology from her team should impress you even further!

There's more???

Yes! Smart Biodetection.

Valuable Waste

Synthetic Biology employs the latest technology to transform organic waste from homes and farms into biofuels such as gasoline, butane and propane. That is how "trash" is converted to "treasure".

SYNTHETIC BIOLOGY

Clean, Green Scientist

Technology for the detectives?

I guess you could say that. Or you could also say that this technology makes us all detectives!

Biodetection helps us detect harmful materials such as diseases or pesticides.

That helps us destroy them and stop them from spreading!

Wow, I guess I was wrong about science and technology being bad for our environment.

Thanks to Dr Pimchai Chaiyen!

Exactly! Cool, huh?

Clean, Green Scientist

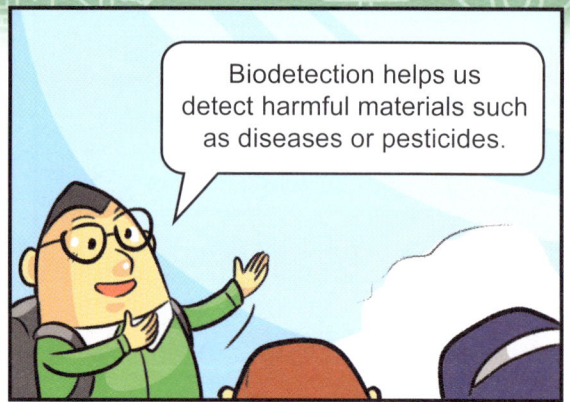

Tactical Technology

Smart Biodetection involves the emission of blue, green or orange light based on the reactions of enzymes. They can be used to identify toxic matter such as pesticides and herbicides in the environment or in agricultural products.

The Achievements of Dr Pimchai Chaiyen

Dr Pimchai Chaiyen has achieved many notable milestones in her life. Here are just some of them.

Education

In 1992, she graduated with First Class Honours for her bachelor's degree in Chemistry from Prince of Songkla University in Thailand. She then received her PhD in Biological Chemistry from the University of Michigan in the USA in 1997.

Awards and Distinctions

In 1985, Dr Chaiyen received the Distinguished Student Award from Princess Sirindhorn.
In 2015, she was the Outstanding Scientist of Thailand, receiving the award from the Foundation for the Promotion of Science and Technology under the patronage of the King of Thailand.
In 2020, she received the Research Excellence Award from the National Research Council of Thailand.

Articles and Lectures

Dr Chaiyen has written more than 100 published articles for renowned journals. She has also been invited to give lectures at more than 50 symposiums worldwide.

Papa Algebra?

A nice night for stargazing, eh?

Yes Dad! Look, it's the Little Dipper looking radiant as always.

The "Little Bear" certainly seems to be smiling at you, son!

So, what was the cause of the hair-tearing?

Oh, you saw that?

It's just…Maths.

Ah, I understand. When I was your age, I found Maths mesmerising… in a confusing way.

Really? You too, Dad? I always thought you were good in Maths!

Papa Algebra?

Not all the time! Can you guess which topic I dreaded most?

The Little Bear

The Little Dipper is formed by seven bright stars (including Polaris, the North Star) in the shape of a ladle, which explains its name. It is found in the constellation Ursa Minor which is affectionately known as the Little Bear.

Ursa Minor

Ursa Major

Papa Algebra?

What was it?

Algebra!

No way!!! That's what I'm struggling with too! I must have inherited the Algebra-confusion from you, Dad!

Ha ha! I'm not sure if that can be passed down.

Anyway, I used to really dislike the person who came up with Algebra: Muhammad ibn Musa al-Khwarizmi.

So, he's the one who has given us all this grief?

While that may be true, he's actually quite the hero!

Why do you say that?

Persian Polymath
Born in the year 780, Muhammad ibn Musa al-Khwarizmi accomplished most of his work in 813-833. He worked in the House of Wisdom in Baghdad, a centre of scientific studies and trade. Al-Khwarizmi was appointed as the astronomer and head of the library at the House of Wisdom.

Well, Muhammad ibn Musa al-Khwarizmi contributed greatly to the world of Mathematics and Science.

He introduced the systematic solving of linear and quadratic equations in his book titled The Compendious Book on Calculation by Completion and Balancing.

He wanted to offer practical solutions to everyday problems. So, his book explained how to use equations to split an inheritance, divide a plot of land, and even find measurements for canals and buildings.

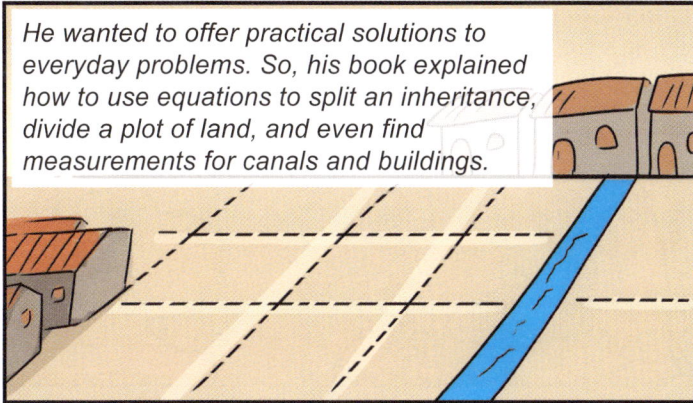

Wow, his people must have considered him a hero!

Not just his people. Translations of his book were introduced to the Western world in the 12th century.

What's more, it was used as the main mathematical textbook in European universities!

How Algebra was Named
The term 'algebra' comes from the title of the book by al-Khwarizmi, *The Compendious Book on Calculation by Completion and Balancing.* The word 'al-jabr' (which sounds like algebra) means 'completion'.

So, he was a master teacher of algebra.

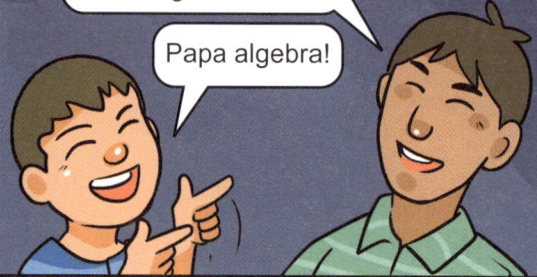

Some people even call him the "father of algebra".

Papa algebra!

Not just that. He's also known as the "grandfather of algorithms" because his findings opened the way to a study of algorithms.

You mean, the algorithms we use to programme our robots today? Cool!

Papa Algebra?

Yes! In fact, the word "algorithm" was taken from his name!

This guy is just getting cooler and cooler!

Algorithms in Robotics

We use algorithms to describe a procedure for controlling the workspace for a robot. When a robot receives Artificial Intelligence (AI) algorithms, it is able to work on its own after a "trial-and-error training phase". It does not need to receive orders to make a decision.

Well, since you're into cool facts, here's another one that might interest you!

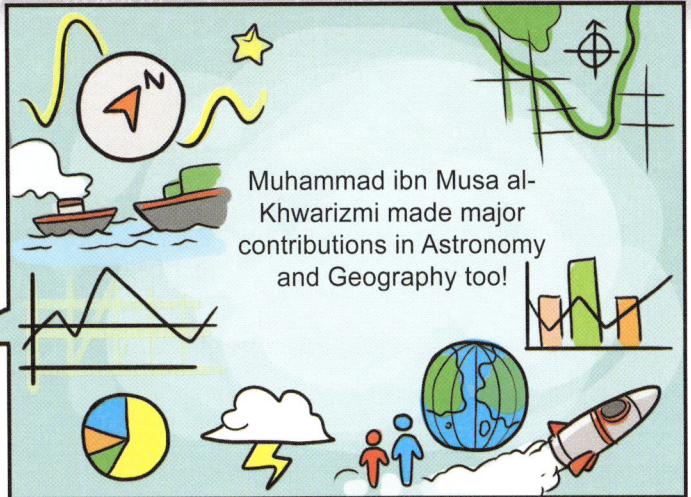

Muhammad ibn Musa al-Khwarizmi made major contributions in Astronomy and Geography too!

Astronomy? My favourite subject! What did he do?

He produced the "Astronomical tables of Siddhanta", which contain information on calendars and astronomy. Among other interesting information, these tables tell us about how the sun, moon and planets move!

Wow, I am so impressed. And inspired! I didn't know that the guy who gave us algebra was also an astronomy fan, like me!

Ha ha yes, you could say that.

I can't disappoint Mr al-Khwarizmi then. Let me go try harder to understand his algebra!

73

Papa Algebra?

Dabbling in Varied Fields

Muhammad ibn Musa al-Khwarizmi was most well-known for his contributions in Algebra and Mathematics. But he had significant contributions in other fields as well.

Astronomy

Al-Khwarizmi wrote a 37-chapter book titled Astronomical tables of Siddhanta. It contains data and calculations for calendars and astronomy as well as a table of sine values. The book contains tables for the movements of the sun, the moon and the five planets known at that time.

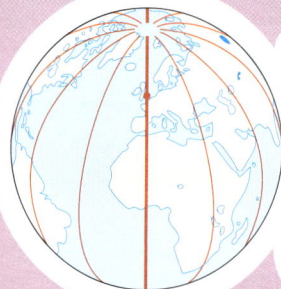

Geography

In 833, Al-Khwarizmi finished writing Book of the Description of the Earth. It contains a list of 2402 coordinates of cities and a list of latitudes and longitudes, both of which help others make important deductions in geography.

Lines of longitude

Lines of latitude

Sundial Improvement

The sundial is an instrument used to show the time, with the help of the sun's position. Al-Khwarizmi made major improvements to this ancient device, making it useable around the world for checking the time.

Papa Algebra?

As Clear as a Bell

RINNGG~

Hello?

It's your precious daughter!

Ha ha, what's up?

I need your advice, Mum!

Are you in some kind of trouble, Kae?

No way! It's just that I'm at this Learning Fair and I'm wondering what I should sign up for.

As Clear as a Bell

Why not? The person who invented the thing you're holding now did that.

The phone? Who?

Alexander Graham Bell! He had quite a few pursuits.

Bell had an active mind. While playing at his neighbour's flour mill…

Dehusking wheat grains is such a boring and laborious task!

Is that so?

Bell built a dehusking device for his neighbour's flour mill. He was only 12 then.

Later, he invented one of the first metal detectors in the world. He also developed hydrofoil boats and motor-powered aircraft.

As Clear as a Bell

Boat with a Boost

One of Alexander Graham Bell's most famous hydrofoil boats was the HD-4. It was fast, stable and powered by Renault engines. The HD-4 set a world marine speed record of 114 kilometres per hour in 1919, a record which stood for 10 years.

Bell also conducted extensive experiments with the breeding of rams and ewes.

Sheep breeding is fascinating!

Those are such different fields! And all along, I thought he had devoted his whole life to developing the telephone.

Oh no! He even played the piano!

Wow Mum, that's amazing. Okay, I'll sign up for ALL the courses then. A warning, though…it won't come cheap!

Sure, but I'll be expecting results. Maybe… a robot that can bring me the delicious pies that you've baked while singing a song that you've composed.

Hahaha sure, Mum! Bye!!!

Bye, dear.

ZZZZZZ-

As Clear as a Bell

The Telephone – A Family-inspired Invention

Alexander Graham Bell is credited with the invention of the telephone. But not many people know that some conditions in his family provided the main foundations for this invention.

Born on 3 March 1847 in Edinburgh, Scotland, Alexander Graham Bell came from a family that was closely associated with elocution, the skill of clear and expressive speech, achieved through distinct pronunciation. As elocutionists, they studied sounds in great depth. His father, Alexander Melville Bell, created a system of symbols (called Visible Speech) to represent the position of the speech organs when producing various sounds. The family trained deaf-mutes to articulate words and read lip movements to understand meaning.

Bell's first telephone

Alexander Graham Bell

Bell's mother began to lose her hearing when he was 12 years old. She would gradually become deaf over the following years. He learnt a finger language so that he could tap out family conversations to his mother while seated at her side. He also developed a technique of speaking directly into his mother's forehead so she could hear him rather clearly.

Both his family background (as experts in sound), and the desire to help his mother, contributed to the invention of the telephone. Bell learnt to use his knowledge and apply it wisely to an area of need.

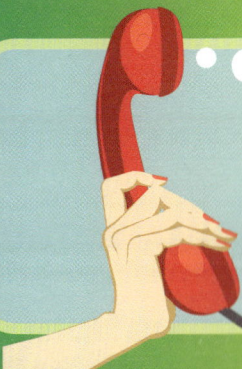

Hello

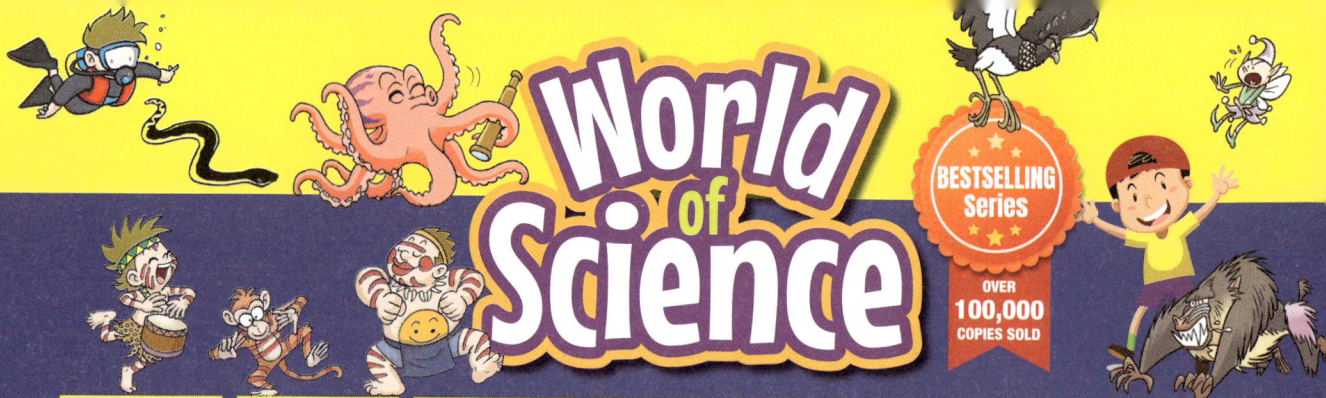

The *World of Science* series engages, educates and entertains children, imparting scientific facts, while nurturing the love of Science through dynamic, full-colour comics. All topics covered are in line with the Singapore primary Science syllabus and the Cambridge primary Science curriculum, and also offer beyond-the-syllabus insights designed to stretch inquiring young minds.